GLASS OF THE ROMAN EMPIRE

DAVID WHITEHOUSE

THE CORNING MUSEUM OF GLASS

Copyright © 1988
The Corning Museum of Glass
Corning, New York 14830–2253

Printed in U.S.A.
Standard Book Number 0–87290–118–1
Library of Congress Catalog Card Number 88–70185

Design: Mary Lou Littrell
Photography: Nicholas L. Williams and Raymond F. Errett
Printed by Village Craftsmen, Inc./Princeton Polychrome Press

CONTENTS

Preface 4

Introduction 5

Illustrations 9

Glossary 58

Further Reading 60

PREFACE

THIS BOOK IS in two parts. The first part traces the history of Roman glassmaking between about 100 B.C. and about A.D. 500—from before the Romans completed their conquest of the Mediterranean until after their empire began to collapse. The second part illustrates 24 outstanding examples of Roman glass in The Corning Museum of Glass and describes the methods that were used to make them. The glossary on pages 58–59 explains the names of glassmakers' tools and techniques. At the end of the volume, there is a list of books and articles that discuss the Roman Empire and the achievements of its glassmakers.

For nearly 500 years, from the first century B.C. to the fifth century A.D., the Romans ruled one of the largest empires that had ever existed. At its greatest extent, the Roman Empire reached from the Atlantic Ocean to the Arabian or Persian Gulf, and from the Rhine to the Sahara Desert. It occupied 1,750,000 square miles and had a population of about 50 million. Rome itself supported a million inhabitants, and four other cities—Alexandria, Antioch, Carthage, and (later) Constantinople—each had 100,000 or more. There had never been a larger city in Europe than Imperial Rome, and some of its monuments are standing today, after more than 1,500 years.

Ancient Rome left us an immense legacy. Christianity, which in the fourth century became the official religion of the Roman Empire, today has more than a billion adherents. Roman law is the basis of the legal systems of many modern countries. In the 15th century, the rediscovery of Roman art and literature led directly to the Renaissance.

Nevertheless, by our standards, the economy and the technology of the Roman Empire were essentially primitive. Even in Italy, at the heart of the empire, the economy was based on agriculture and the overwhelming majority of the population worked on the land. Stephen Dyson, a classical archeologist who also studies historic sites in the United States, compares the Roman countryside with New England before the Industrial Revolution. Roman Italy and 18th-century New England, he writes, were lands of "peasants, peddlers, shop keepers and merchants with an economy tied into the emerging world system, but at the same time regional and even local in many of its qualities."[1]

This is the background against which Roman glassmaking developed. The very rich—a tiny minority of the total population—commissioned luxury objects such as cameo glasses (Fig. 8) and cage cups (Fig. 21). City dwellers, like those members of the rural population who lived within reach of markets and produced surpluses which they could barter or sell, acquired glass vessels as well as foodstuffs and patent medicines in glass containers. A smaller number bought glass to glaze their windows. For the first time in history, glass was no longer exclusively a luxury product, and inexpensive items were available in every province of the empire.

In the pages that follow, particular attention is paid to luxury items, which display the skills of the Roman glassmakers at their best. We should not forget, however, that for every luxury object, there were hundreds—perhaps thousands—of vessels for everyday use.

---

1. Stephen Dyson, "The Villa of Buccino and the Consumer Model of Roman Rural Development," in *Papers in Italian Archaeology, v. 4, The Cambridge Conference*, edited by Caroline Malone and Simon Stoddart. Oxford: British Archaeological Reports, 1985, part 4, pp. 67–84, especially p. 79.

INTRODUCTION

THE PEOPLES OF the Roman Empire used a greater quantity and variety of glass than any other civilization before the Renaissance. They made dazzling luxury glass for the tables of the rich. They discovered glassblowing and, as a result, inexpensive glass vessels became widely available. They made the world's first window glass and decorated the interiors of buildings with glass mosaics and panels. Glass beads, rings, and hairpins were common, as were gaming pieces and mirrors. Roman authors wrote of magnifying glasses, glass statues, and even glass that was unbreakable.[2]

Glassmaking, however, did not begin with the Romans. The earliest man-made glass had been produced more than 2,000 years before the founding of the Roman Empire. By 1500 B.C., craftsmen in Mesopotamia and Egypt were making small, brightly colored vessels by winding threads of molten glass around a removable core. Another early technique was to create a "mosaic" effect by covering the core with preformed canes,[3] which then were fused by heating. Larger, open forms were first produced in Mesopotamia in the eighth century B.C. These vessels were made by casting blanks in a mold and finished by grinding and polishing. Unlike many of the earlier products, they were monochrome, usually translucent bluish green or amber (the natural colors of man-made glass). Shortly afterward, glassmakers discovered that the addition to the batch of a small quantity of antimony or manganese would remove all trace of green or amber, leaving the glass colorless.

Glassmaking spread from western Asia to the eastern and central Mediterranean in the seventh and sixth centuries B.C. In the eastern Mediterranean, production expanded and diversified after the late fourth century. Alexandria in Egypt became a well-known center of glassmaking. Other centers are known to have existed in Syria, in Palestine, and on the island of Rhodes, where a beadmaker's workshop has been discovered. Glassmakers produced core-formed bottles and miniature pitchers for perfumes and other cosmetics, as well as a wide range of cast, ground, and wheel-cut tableware. Some vessels were colorless, while others were brightly colored. The latter included mosaic glass, often with lace-like and ribbon patterns, and the first "gold-sandwich" glass, which was decorated with gold foil sandwiched between two closely fitting vessels which were reheated until they fused. Nevertheless, although glass was produced in ever-increasing quantities, it remained a luxury item. Making a mosaic glass bowl required days of work by a team of craftsmen, and the product was priced accordingly.

Meanwhile, in Italy, luxury glass was available in the Greek cities of the south, and small core-formed vessels were made farther north in Etruria. Rome itself, however, was neither a producer nor a significant importer of glass until the first century B.C.

In the mid-first century B.C., glassmaking was transformed by the discovery that glass can be blown. As a result of this discovery, by the time of Christ, glass had ceased to be exclusively a luxury item, and craftsmen were producing inexpensive objects for everyday use. "At Rome," wrote Strabo, "a bowl or a drinking cup may be purchased for a copper coin."[4] Neither Strabo nor Pliny (the writer who tells us the most about Roman glassmaking) reveals where the new technique originated, and we must rely on archeological discoveries to determine where and when it occurred. Some of the earliest blown glass known to us comes from Syria and Palestine, and finds from Israel strongly suggest that glass-blowing was discovered about 50 B.C. From this moment, glassmakers in the eastern Mediterranean were able to make thin-walled, transparent vessels quickly and in a vast range of shapes and sizes. The increase in production is evident from the large numbers of glass fragments found in excavations of Roman sites and from the number of times glass was mentioned by Roman writers in the first century A.D.

In the reign of the first Roman emperor, Augustus (27 B.C.–A.D. 14), glassmakers established themselves in Rome and other parts of Italy. At first, the new workshops specialized in vessels cast in molds. Excavations in Rome and at other sites show that monochrome vessels were common; translucent green and blue, and opaque white and red were four of the most popular colors. Among the forms were cups which copied the shapes of contemporary silver and bronze vessels (Fig. 1). A unique cast and wheel-cut cover in the form of a fish (Fig. 2) is probably of similar date. In the *Satyricon* of Petronius, the fictional character Trimalchio explains that he prefers glass to bronze for vessels used with food and drink because it does not smell, and he adds that he would prefer glass to gold if only it were less fragile.[5]

At the same time, Italian workshops also produced local versions of the polychrome vessels first made in the eastern Mediterranean. These included mosaic glass (millefiori) made from preformed canes usually of two or more colors (Fig. 3); lace mosaic glass *(reticelli)*, in which canes containing twisted threads of colored glass were fused to form a disk, then softened in the furnace and sagged over "former" molds to make shallow bowls; ribbon mosaic glass, in which glass strips of different colored glass were arranged in geometric patterns, and then fused and sagged in the same way as *reticelli* vessels (Fig. 4); and gold-band glass, which contained strips of gold foil between layers of colorless glass (Fig. 5).

After the mid-first century A.D., cast and colored glass declined in popularity. Neither was abandoned, however, and a cast figurine of Venus (Fig. 6) probably dates from the second century. Mosaic glass perhaps continued to be used for interior decoration (Fig. 7), and the production of cameo glass (Fig. 8)—one of the high points of Roman glassmaking—may have continued for a decade or so after A.D. 50.

By this time, however, the overwhelming majority of glass vessels were made by blowing (Fig. 9) and, among them, a high proportion was of naturally colored or colorless glass. Colorless glass began to attract attention between about A.D. 50 and 75. Pliny, writing in about 77, provides a clear indication of this. "The most highly valued glass," he wrote, "is colorless and transparent, resembling rock crystal as closely as possible. . . . Glassware has now come to resemble rock crystal in a remarkable manner and the value of the former has increased without reducing the value of the latter."[6]

During the first century A.D., glassmakers set up workshops in the western and northern provinces. Pliny mentions glassmaking in Spain and Gaul, and before the end of the century glass was also being made in Britain and Germany.

The rise of glassblowing was accompanied by new techniques of decorating the glass while it was hot. These included the application of blobs or trails. In the first century, chips or blobs of opaque white and colored glass were applied to the walls of brightly colored flasks, bowls, and cups, and they were either marvered flush with the surface, thereby creating a splashed or streaky effect (Fig. 10), or left projecting from the vessel. Later, a different effect was achieved by applying trails bent into "snake-thread" designs; some of these designs were purely abstract and others included birds or fish (Fig. 11). Yet another technique was to apply vertical trails, which were nipped together to form a lattice in low relief (Fig. 12).

By the early first century A.D., the Romans had also discovered that glass can be formed by blowing it into decorated molds. This discovery made possible the production of vessels with designs similar to those found on contemporary relief-decorated metal without the laborious business of casting and cutting them on the lathe or wheel. Most of the glass produced by blowing into molds was either tableware such as beakers, cups, and pitchers, or containers for cosmetics. Many of these objects were hastily produced in inexpensive greenish or amber glass, but others were exceptionally handsome and presumably commanded exceptional prices. Some of the finest vessels of all were signed by Ennion, who appears to have worked first in Syria and later in northern Italy (Fig. 13).

Among the earliest mold-blown drinking vessels were beakers with designs depicting gods and heroes from Greco-Roman mythology (Fig. 14). In the western provinces, gladiators and charioteers, usually identified by name, were popular subjects (Fig. 15). Unusual shapes included flasks in the form of a human head (Fig. 17). Later, mold-blown vessels might be decorated with Christian or Jewish motifs (Fig. 18).

In the first four centuries A.D., the most popular method of decorating glass vessels when they were cold was by cutting and engraving. Wheel-cut decoration varied in complexity from simple horizontal grooves to faceting to pictorial designs with figures, landscapes, and inscriptions. Some of the earliest examples, made in the late first and early second centuries, have overall patterns of intersecting facets. Following a break in production which lasted until around the end of the second century, objects displaying scenes with figures appeared; this glass was decorated with a combination of facet-cutting and engraving.

In the fourth century, cutting and engraving were widely used—in Rome, in Cologne, in Egypt, and elsewhere—to produce hunting scenes, episodes from pagan mythology, and Christian motifs such as the miracle of Christ healing the paralytic (Fig. 19). In addition to crisp linear cutting, some decorators used abrasion, which derived its effect from the contrast between the dullness of the abraded areas and the brilliance of the rest of the surface (Fig. 20).

The most spectacular of all Roman wheel-cut vessels are the cage cups of the late third and early fourth centuries. These rank among the most accomplished achievements of glass cutting in any time or place (Fig. 21). Each cage cup was made from a single thick-walled blank which was cut to produce free-standing figures, inscriptions, or "cages" of adjoining meshes attached to the body of the vessel by struts or posts. We know that one cage cup, found at Strasbourg in the last century, was made for a Roman emperor, and it is probable that most vessels of this type were owned by rich aristocrats and members of the imperial entourage.

One of the least-documented Roman methods of decorating glass vessels was painting. Few objects have survived intact, and it is likely that many examples have perished because the paint became detached as the surface of the glass deteriorated. Among the varieties of painted vessels that do survive are a group of tableware datable to the second and third quarters of the first century A.D.; lidded jars made in Cyprus in the second century; cups decorated with circus scenes and wild animals, attributed to the late second and third centuries; and other vessels, including the Daphne Ewer (Fig. 22), which seem to have been made in the eastern provinces in the third or fourth centuries.

The luxury glass of the Hellenistic period had included objects in which gold foil was sandwiched between two almost identical vessels which had been fused. A similar effect was achieved in the third and fourth centuries, when gold-foil medallions became popular as the centerpieces of dishes and bowls, the bases of which were frequently displayed in the Roman catacombs (Fig. 23). An unusual variation on the "gold sandwich" theme is illustrated by a two-handled cup known as the Disch Kantharos, on which the decoration is rendered on the outside in gold foil and protected from wear by a "cage" of zigzag trails (Fig. 24).

When the western provinces of the Roman Empire collapsed in the fifth century, glassmaking (in common with other crafts) declined, and all but the simplest techniques were forgotten. A decline also occurred in the East, but it was less severe. Mold-blown vessels continued to be made in Syria and Palestine, and perhaps also in Egypt. Nevertheless, from one end of the Mediterranean to the other, the golden age of Roman glassmaking was over.

2. Accounts of unbreakable glass appear in the writings of Petronius and Pliny the Elder. But, as Pliny remarked, "The story was told ... with greater frequency than truth." (*Natural History*, 36.66.197). Petronius, a close adviser of the emperor Nero, died in A.D. 66. Pliny the Elder wrote a 37-book encyclopedia known as the *Natural History*. He died in the eruption of Vesuvius, which destroyed Pompeii in A.D. 79.
3. For this and other glassmaking terms, see the glossary on pp. 58–59.
4. David F. Grose, "Early Blown Glass. The Western Evidence," *Journal of Glass Studies*, v. 19, 1977, pp. 9–29, especially pp. 13–14, quoting Strabo, *Geography*, 16.2.25. Strabo died about A.D. 21.
5. Petronius, *Satyricon*, 50.
6. Pliny, *Natural History*, 37.10.29.

ILLUSTRATIONS

THE 24 OBJECTS are arranged according to the techniques used to form or finish them. Figures 1–7 show objects made by techniques inherited from pre-Roman glassmakers: casting, lathe cutting, grinding, and polishing. Figure 8 is an example of cameo glass. Figure 9 and most (perhaps all) of the remaining illustrations show objects formed by blowing.

The Romans employed a variety of methods to decorate blown glass. While it was hot, they applied glass as random fragments (Fig. 10) or trails (Figs. 11 and 12), and they blew elaborately decorated forms in molds (Figs. 13–18). When the glass was cold, they cut and engraved it (Figs. 19–21). The Romans also painted glass (Fig. 22) and applied designs cut out of gold foil (Figs. 23–24).

UNTIL THE DISCOVERY of glassblowing, the glass-makers of the Roman Empire relied on techniques perfected in the Hellenistic world of the eastern Mediterranean. These included fusing sections of glass canes around a preformed core, grinding from a block or "blank," and casting in molds. When casting, early glassmakers had to contend with two practical problems. First, molten glass is far less fluid than molten metal, and it is difficult to fill every cavity in a mold simply by pouring. Second, this difficulty was aggravated by the problem of keeping the molten glass sufficiently hot during the casting process.

Roman glassmakers knew several methods of avoiding these difficulties. When casting in a closed mold, they sometimes packed it with finely powdered glass, which was fused by placing the mold in a furnace. When using an open mold, they sometimes forced the viscous glass into position with a tool or perhaps a plunger, and sometimes placed a slab of glass over the mold, and heated the glass until it became soft and slumped into place. However they were formed, objects were annealed (cooled slowly) and finished by using a lathe to cut and grind away irregularities or by reheating to create a shiny "fire-polished" effect.

Fig. 1

Cup with two handles, cast, lathe-cut, and wheel-cut. Eastern Mediterranean or Italy, mid- to late 1st century B.C. H. 9.6 cm ($3^{25}/_{32}$ in). 70.1.29.

This remarkable vessel was cut from a single cast blank; there is no evidence that the handles were secondary applications. Indeed, traces exist of cutting and grinding at oblique angles to the handles, and there is also a marked thickening in the vessel wall around the handle junctures. The form imitates silverware. Two small drilled holes near one handle indicate an ancient repair.

IN ADDITION TO vessels with conventional shapes, such as a cup with two handles (Fig. 1) which also occurs in silver and the bowls (Figs. 3–4) which also occur in earthenware, Roman glassmakers sometimes produced objects in unexpected and highly original forms. The fish shown on the opposite page is one such object. This unique piece is one of the treasures of the Roman collection at The Corning Museum of Glass. It was cast in a mold. The upper surface was polished and wheel-cut with realistic (and anatomically correct) details: mouth, eye, gills, fins, and so on. The underside is hollow, and the only "details" consist of groups of parallel cuts on the fins and tail. Clearly, only the upper surface was meant to be seen, and it is assumed that the object was a lid—the cover of a dish for serving fish. One lifted the glass fish (the cuts on the underside of the fins and tail would have made a firm grip possible) and found the real fish (about the size of a trout) resting on the dish.

Fig. 2
Cover in the form of a fish, cast, wheel-cut, polished. Probably Italy, 1st century A.D. L. 33.7 cm (13 5/16 in). 67.1.1.

IN THE THIRD century B.C., glassmakers in the eastern Mediterranean revived the ancient craft of making mosaic glass, and this remained one of the most sought-after varieties of luxury glass until the early first century A.D.

Mosaic glass takes its name from the manner in which objects are fashioned from a mosaic of multicolored rods and canes. The glassmaker first prepared a selection of colored rods (each made from a single gob of glass) or canes (composite elements made from rods of different colors fused by heating). These were then cut into pieces, either like slices of salami or in short longitudinal sections. Vessels were formed by placing the pieces side by side on the inner surface of a mold. A second mold was inserted above them in order to hold the pieces in position. Next, the mold was heated in a furnace. The canes became soft and, on cooling, fused to form a vessel with the same shape as the mold. Irregularities could be concealed by adding extra pieces of glass and reheating, after which a spirally wound trail of contrasting colors was applied to form the rim. The last stage in the manufacturing process consisted of smoothing the surface by grinding and polishing on a lathe and by fire-polishing.

Fig. 3
Mosaic-glass bowl. Preformed canes fused in or on mold, interior lathe-polished, exterior fire-polished. Eastern Mediterranean, first half of 1st century B.C. D. 13.2 cm (5³⁄₁₆ in). 55.1.81.

Two holes have been drilled in the wall just below the rim, possibly to attach a cover.

A NEW VARIETY of mosaic glass was introduced in the first century B.C. This was "ribbon" mosaic, and the ornament consisted mainly of lengths (not slices) of rods and canes arranged in geometric patterns. The earliest closely dated ribbon-glass vessel was found by divers among the remains of a ship which sank off the island of Antikythera, halfway between Crete and the Greek mainland, sometime between about 80 and 50 B.C.

The object from the Antikythera wreck is a dish made from parallel canes. This simple arrangement was copied by glassmakers in Italy, who began to produce ribbon-mosaic glass toward the end of the first century B.C. Soon, however, they were also making more complex designs in which the ornament was divided into quadrants, each filled with canes laid at right angles.

Unlike other varieties of mosaic glass, which were made by arranging the components in a mold, ribbon glass was probably produced by arranging them side by side on a flat surface and fusing them to form a disk. The disk was placed on a convex former mold and heated until the glass softened and slumped over the mold, thereby forming a hollow vessel. The glassmaker then applied a softened spirally twisted cane to make the rim, and he finished the object by grinding and polishing or by fire-polishing.

Ribbon-mosaic glass is brilliantly colored, and the example illustrated here includes sections from rods of six different colors (yellowish green, deep blue, amber, amethyst, yellow, and opaque white) and three composite canes (amethyst with an opaque white twist, colorless with a yellow twist, and, at the center, one slice from a complex arrangement of yellow, amethyst, blue, and white). The fashion for brightly colored glass lasted until the mid-first century A.D., after which it declined and colorless glass gained in popularity (see Fig. 11).

Fig. 4
Ribbon-glass bowl. Preformed rods and canes fused in or on mold. Italy, late 1st century B.C.–early 1st century A.D. D. 13.5 cm (5 5/16 in). 66.1.214.

This bowl was found near Adria in northern Italy.

GOLD-BAND GLASS is the most exotic variant of ribbon-mosaic glass. The name refers to the presence of strips of gold foil laminated between ribbons of transparent, usually colorless glass. It is still not known precisely how gold-band vessels were formed. Perhaps groups of ribbons were first fused in sinuous patterns, after which the fused units were laid side by side in a mold, fused again, and pushed into shape by tooling. After annealing, vessels were finished by grinding away irregularities and cutting the grooves that accentuate the profile.

Gold-band glass was made first by Hellenistic glassmakers in the eastern Mediterranean. It is generally agreed, however, that two of the most common varieties, miniature bottles (such as the vessel on the opposite page) and cylindrical boxes with lids, were made in Italy in the first century A.D.

Fig. 5
Gold-band bottle. Preformed sections perhaps cast on core, manipulated, cast again, and lathe-cut. Probably Italy, early to mid-1st century A.D. H. 7.3 cm (2⅞ in). 59.1.87.

THIS IS A rare example of Roman miniature sculpture in glass. It was probably cast by the "lost wax" technique, a method first used for casting metal. The object was modeled in wax, encased in clay or plaster, and then heated. The wax melted and was released through vents or "gates," also made of wax, which had been attached to the object before it was encased. At the same time, the clay or plaster dried and became rigid. This then served as a mold, into which molten or more probably powdered glass was introduced through the gates. If powdered glass was used, the mold was heated in order to fuse the contents. After cooling, the object was removed from the mold, annealed, and finished by cutting.

Fig. 6

Figurine of Venus, cast, with wheel-cut details. Eastern Mediterranean or Italy, probably 2nd century A.D. H. 9.4 cm ($3^{23}/_{32}$ in). 55.1.84.

The figurine is a version of the Aphrodite of Knidos, a Greek life-size marble sculpture of the third century B.C., which was frequently copied by Roman artists in the first and second centuries A.D. Although the figurine was intended to have separate arms, there is no reason to believe that the head and lower legs (now missing) were cast separately. There is a similar figurine in the Museum of Fine Arts, Boston.

The flesh-like color of the surface is the result of a chemical reaction between the glass and its environment, presumably during centuries of burial. When it was new, the object was yellowish green.

THE PLAQUE SHOWN on the opposite page probably was part of a much larger frieze or panel which adorned the wall of a house. It was made by fashioning the birds, branches, and flowers from preformed canes (which were fused in the same way that canes were fused to form mosaic-glass vessels) and embedding them in a matrix of bluish-green glass.

The same subject occurs in Roman wall paintings such as those which adorned the garden room in the house of Livia (the wife of the emperor Augustus) at Prima Porta, a few miles north of Rome. Pliny the Younger, writing to a friend between A.D. 104 and 108, described one such painting in his Tuscan villa: "The walls are covered with marble up to the cornice; on the frieze above, foliage is painted, with birds perched among the branches" (*Letters* 5.6).

Fig. 7
Mosaic-glass plaque with birds among branches. Mosaic glass fused in glass matrix. Probably Italy, perhaps 1st century A.D. H. (without modern frame) 26.5 cm (10⁷⁄₁₆ in). 66.1.215.

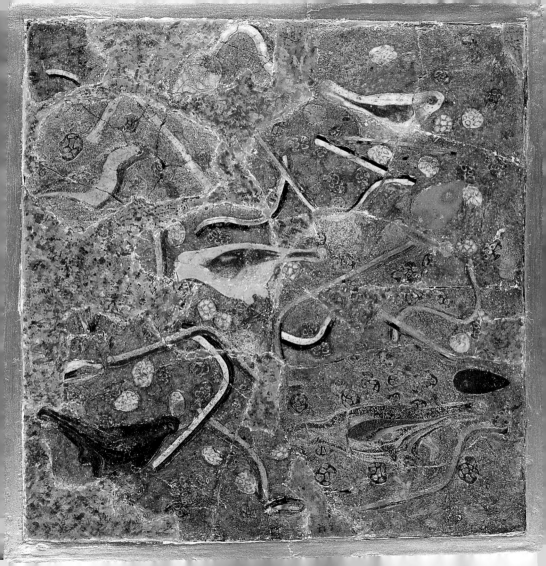

THE RAREST AND most elaborate luxury vessels of the early Roman Empire are cameo glasses, objects inspired by relief-cut gems of banded semiprecious stones such as onyx. Glassmakers "cased" (that is, covered) objects of one color with one or more layers of glass of different colors, opaque white on translucent deep blue being the most popular combination. After casing, the layered "blank" was given to a lapidary for carving, cutting, and polishing. Using hand tools and a rotating wheel fed with abrasive, the lapidary removed most of the overlay, leaving the ornament in low relief. The process required not only skill but also a great deal of time; when, in 1876, John Northwood completed the first glass replica of the Portland Vase (the most famous ancient cameo-glass vessel), it had taken three years of concentrated activity.

It is frequently maintained that the first cameo glasses were made in Egypt, perhaps as early as the fourth century B.C. It is much more likely, however, regardless of where they were made, that the earliest examples belong to the second half of the first century B.C. Indeed, most cameo glasses probably were made in Italy between about 25 B.C. and A.D. 50 or 60. At least five examples have been found at Pompeii, one of the cities destroyed by the eruption of Vesuvius in A.D. 79.

Fig. 8
The Morgan Cup, cast or blown, wheel-cut, engraved. Probably Italy, late 1st century B.C. H. 6.2 cm (2⁷⁄₁₆ in). 52.1.93, gift of Arthur A. Houghton, Jr.

The cup is decorated with a continuous frieze depicting a religious ceremony at a rural shrine. A satyr is fastening a curtain to the top of a column to insure privacy, while a female attendant uncovers a basket of offerings. On the other side, a second female with an attendant approaches a statue of Silenus. In Greek mythology, Silenus was the tutor of the god Dionysus. Women who wanted to become pregnant or to have an easy confinement sometimes invoked the help of Dionysus, for whom Silenus here acts as proxy.

AFTER THE DISCOVERY of glass itself, the most important innovation in the history of glassmaking was the discovery that glass can be blown. This simplified and speeded up the production of glass vessels. As a result, glass ceased to be exclusively a luxury item, and simple glassware became relatively inexpensive. Although never as cheap as earthenware, glass vessels had several advantages: they were easy to clean, they did not impart an odor to their contents, and they allowed one to see the contents even when the vessel was sealed.

Although glassblowing requires considerable skill on the part of the glassmaker, the principle of this technique is very simple. Using an iron blowpipe three to five feet long, the worker gathers from the pot in the furnace a gob of molten glass. After slightly inflating the gob, he manipulates it into the desired shape by swinging it, rolling it on a marver (a smooth, flat surface), or shaping it with tools. The gob is then blown into the final shape and tooled as necessary. After this, it is removed from the blowpipe so that the neck and rim can be finished by further tooling. For this purpose, a solid iron rod called a pontil is attached to the bottom of the vessel with a wad of molten glass.

The earliest evidence of blown glass comes from two sites in Israel. At Ein Gedi, on the western shore of the Dead Sea, a single blown flask was found in the excavation of burial caves near a settlement which is thought to have been abandoned between 40 and 31 B.C. In Jerusalem, small blown unguent bottles were found among debris from a glassmaker's workshop. The workshop in the Jewish Quarter of the Old City had been covered by a floor of about 40 B.C. These two finds lead one to suppose that glassblowing originated somewhere in Syria or Palestine about 40 B.C.

Fig. 9
Container in the form of a bird, blown. Probably northern Italy, second or third quarter of the 1st century A.D. L. (including restored tip of tail) 11.7 cm (4$^{15}/_{32}$ in). 66.1.223.

The container was closed by fusing the tip of the tail, which had to be broken to remove the contents. Some examples contain residues of white or pink powder, presumably a cosmetic.

ONE OF THE earliest methods of decorating blown vessels was the application of random fragments of colored glass to produce a speckled effect. This was achieved by reheating the vessel and either rolling it in loose fragments or dropping the fragments onto it. In both cases, the fragments adhered to the hot surface. The gaffer then had two options: reheating the vessel again to fuse the fragments more firmly to the surface or reheating the vessel and rolling it on a marver (in Roman times, probably a stone slab) until the fragments were flush. If he chose the second option, further inflation could be used to enlarge and distort the flattened fragments, giving the glass a multicolored appearance. It has been suggested that this may have been an inexpensive means of imitating costly mosaic glass such as the bowl in Figure 3.

Glass with a speckled surface seems to have been one of the specialties of the glasshouses of northern Italy in the first century A.D., since excavations on the Po plain and in adjacent regions have brought to light numerous examples. Specimens also occur in the Aegean and around the Black Sea, and this suggests that they were also made in the eastern Mediterranean.

THE NATURAL COLOR of glass is green or amber. This is due to the presence of impurities (mainly iron) in the main ingredient, sand or crushed quartzite. Glassmakers can change the color by adding coloring agents such as cobalt, which produces blue. They can also remove the natural color by adding decolorants. Chemical analyses have revealed that the Romans sometimes used antimony or manganese for this purpose.

The Romans were not the first glassmakers to produce colorless glass. In Hellenistic times, it was already fairly common. Until the first century A.D., however, colored or multicolored vessels were far more popular. After about A.D. 50, colorless glass began to gain ground, although not in all parts of the Empire and not for the simplest utilitarian products. Colorless glass, in fact, came to dominate the upper end of the market, taking the place of colored tableware. The almost colorless beaker shown on the opposite page was decorated by trailing. This was done by reheating the vessel and dropping the decoration on the surface from a gob of molten glass on a pontil. The molten trail was then drawn out and tooled to make the desired pattern.

Fig. 11
Beaker, blown, with applied "snake-thread" decoration of dolphins and water plants. Rhineland, perhaps Cologne, 3rd or early 4th century A.D. H. 20.4 cm (8 1/32 in). 82.1.1.

This beaker was found at Worms in the Federal Republic of Germany.

THIS UNUSUALLY LARGE pitcher with trailed and blobbed decoration was made in the eastern Mediterranean in the fourth century A.D. The decoration was made in the following manner: a thick horizontal trail was applied to the neck and nicked with a rod or pair of pincers. Three vertical zigzag trails were applied to the body and nipped together in a diamond pattern. A small blue blob was applied at the center of each diamond-shaped compartment and in each triangular space below the lowest row of diamonds. The final stage in the manufacturing process was the attachment of the handle.

Fig. 12
Pitcher, blown, with applied and tooled decoration. Syria or Palestine, 4th century A.D. H. 42.5 cm (16⅜ in). 64.1.18.

THE DISCOVERY THAT vessels can be formed and decorated by inflating a gob of glass in a mold permitted the rapid production of large numbers of virtually identical objects. Like glassblowing itself, this discovery was made in the eastern Mediterranean, probably in Syria or Palestine. In the first century A.D., Pliny believed that glassmaking had been invented at Sidon (in modern Lebanon), which in his day was still a famous center of production. For this reason, the earliest mold-blown vessels are frequently described as "Sidonian," although we have no means of telling which, if any, were actually made there.

The finest "Sidonian" Roman vessels bear the signature of Ennion, who seems to have worked first in the eastern Mediterranean and later in northern Italy. The quality of the vessel depended very much on the quality of the mold in which it was blown, and Ennion may have been a particularly skillful moldmaker, rather than the proprietor or gaffer of a glassmaking workshop.

Although mold-blown glass was fairly common in the Roman world, very few fragments of molds have been discovered. All but one of the objects known to me that have been identified as glassmakers' molds are of earthenware, and they seem to have been used for making square bottles (from Cologne, Federal Republic of Germany), flasks shaped like a bunch of grapes (from Macquenoise in Belgium), and cups decorated with scenes of chariot racing (from Borgo in Corsica). The exception, a mold made of copper alloy, may have been used for making hexagonal bottles (now in The Israel Museum, Jerusalem).

Fig. 13
Pitcher signed by Ennion, blown in three-part mold. Eastern Mediterranean, probably Syria or Palestine, 1st century A.D. H. (including handle and restored foot) 23.8 cm (9⅜ in). 59.1.76.

The signature ("Ennion made [it]"), written in Greek, is in a panel underneath the handle.

THIS BEAKER BELONGS to one of the many varieties of mold-blown glass produced in the Mediterranean region in the first and early second centuries A.D. At least 24 examples are known, all of which are decorated with four figures. They have been divided into four groups, each with a different combination of figures. In this case, the figures appear to be gods and heroes from Greek mythology, although their precise identities are uncertain. The date is suggested by finds from archeological excavations. These include two fragments from Masada in Israel, presumably earlier than the destruction of the site in A.D. 73; a fragment from the Roman fort at Vindonissa in Switzerland, which was found in a deposit slightly later than A.D. 60–75; and an example from a late first-century grave at Crnelo, near Ljubljana, in Yugoslavia.

Fig. 14
Beaker, blown in two-part mold. Eastern Mediterranean, late 1st–2nd century A.D. H. 12.6 cm (4³¹/₃₂ in). 68.1.9.

The molded decoration consists of four panels separated by columns. Each panel contains a standing figure; in this case, the figure may be Hercules.

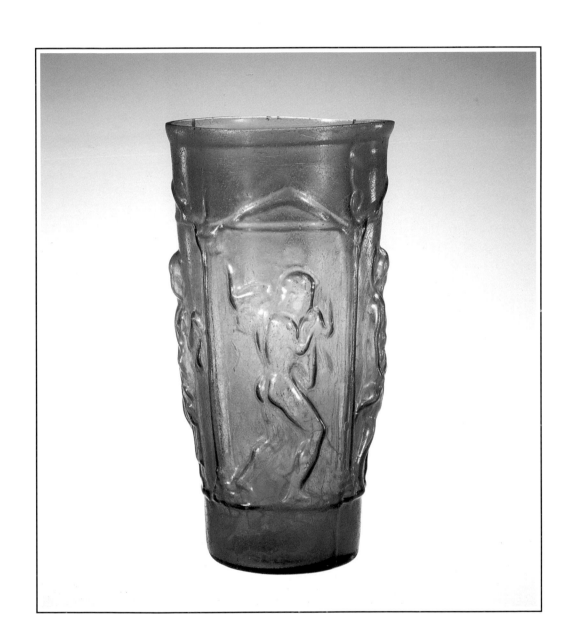

THE EARLIEST MOLD-BLOWN glass known to have been made in the western half of the Roman Empire closely resembles "Sidonian" products from the eastern Mediterranean. Indeed, it includes a series of cups signed by Ennion (see p. 34), who seems to have established or worked at a factory in northern Italy in the mid-first century A.D. The new technique rapidly took hold, and of similar or slightly later date is a large group of mold-blown cups and beakers decorated with gladiatorial contests and chariot racing—two popular sports which drew large crowds to the amphitheater and the circus.

"Sport cups" (as they are called) were blown in two-part molds, with a separate base mold. The decoration, arranged in horizontal bands, includes pairs of fighting gladiators or charioteers and their teams, and inscriptions to identify them. Unlike the sophisticated products of Ennion, many of which were deliberately colored, sport cups are relatively crude and of "natural" green or amber glass. Presumably, therefore, they were modestly priced and intended for the mass market.

Literary references and inscriptions tell us that some of the gladiators named on sport cups fought in Italy, and a strong case has been made for identifying the circus shown on the cups with charioteers as the Circus Maximus in Rome. Nearly all known sport cups, however, were found outside Italy; they are particularly common in the Rhineland, Gaul, and Britain. Their distribution, therefore, suggests that many sport cups were made in the western provinces, but not in Italy. This leads to the conclusion that they were not made to be sold as souvenirs at the events they depict, as is often supposed, but to celebrate sporting heroes whom the purchasers may never have seen in action.

Fig. 15
Beaker with gladiators, blown in two-part mold. Northern Italy or Gaul, mid- to late 1st century A.D. H. 9.6 cm (3 $^{25}/_{32}$ in). 57.1.4, gift of Arthur A. Houghton, Jr.

This beaker, signed by M. Licinius Diceus, shows two pairs of gladiators who are identified by name. The gladiators shown here are Petraites (left) and Prudes, who drops his shield and raises his left hand to acknowledge defeat. Petraites is mentioned by the writer Petronius, who for a time was one of Nero's closest advisers.

The beaker was found at Sopron (Roman Scarbantia), Hungary, in 1892.

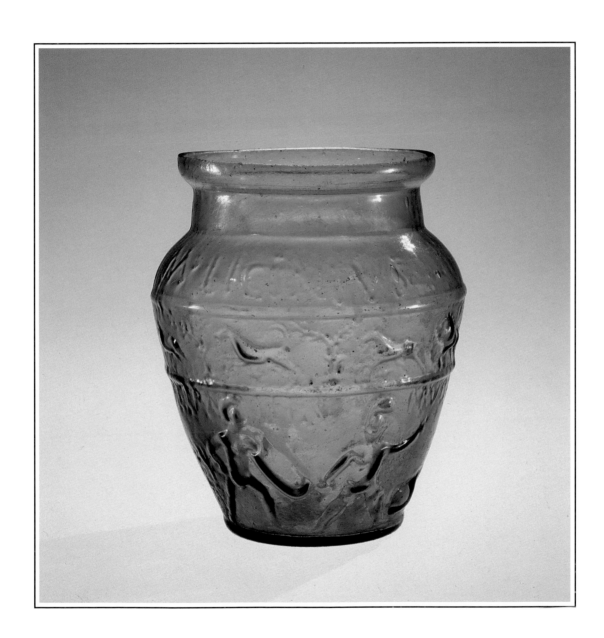

THIS BELL-SHAPED PITCHER was made by blowing a gob of molten glass into a cylindrical mold with vertical ribs. The parison was withdrawn from the mold, reheated, and further inflated. During this process, the body was shaped by tooling, and the vertical ribs were transformed into a spiral pattern by twirling the blowpipe. The handle was made by taking a gob of molten glass on a pontil, dropping it onto the shoulder, drawing it upward and inward, and attaching it to the neck. The remaining part of the gob was then turned back along the upper surface and dragged over the body of the pitcher to form a "tail." Finally, the tail was pincered to produce the ridges.

Fig. 16

Pitcher, body blown in mold, handle applied. Western provinces, probably Gaul, late 1st century A.D. H. 26.1 cm (10⁹/₃₂ in). 85.1.6.

Fewer than 10 intact examples of this unusual form are known.

AFTER THE MID-FOURTH century, glassmaking declined in almost every part of the Roman Empire. In the West, complex objects such as cage cups (Fig. 21) and "gold glasses" (Figs. 23–24) ceased to be made, as did colorless glass and all but the simplest mold-blown vessels. In the East, the decline was less pronounced.

This brilliant blue head flask, made in the eastern Mediterranean in the late fourth or fifth century, was blown in a two-part mold. The handle was made in much the same way as the handle shown in Figure 16, although in this case it was applied first to the neck, then drawn outward and downward, and attached to the head. The remaining glass was dragged down to the neck and notched. The thumb-rest at the apex of the handle was made by pinching the hot glass with pincers. The base consists of a single trail coiled three times around the bottom of the flask to form a foot-ring.

The head flask belongs to a group of late Roman flasks, pitchers, and lamps, most of which are deep blue, mold-blown objects with coiled bases. They seem to have been made in a single workshop, but examples have been found as far afield as the Sudan and South Korea.

Fig. 17
Head flask, blown in two-part mold. Eastern Mediterranean, late 4th or early 5th century A.D. H. 19.6 cm (7²³/₃₂ in). 59.1.150.

Only three other head flasks made from the same mold are known to exist. This example was once in the collection of the celebrated operatic tenor Enrico Caruso (1873–1921).

SOME OF THE most distinctive mold-blown vessels of the late Roman period were made in Syria and Palestine. These are decorated with Christian or Jewish symbols, and many of them are believed to have been made at or near Jerusalem. The pitcher shown on the opposite page belongs to a group of relatively tall vessels, readily distinguishable from the "Jerusalem group" by their height, color, and subject matter. While all but one of the Christian glasses believed to be from Jerusalem are decorated with crosses alternating with large concentric lozenges, the taller vessels also have palm fronds and human figures on columns. The last motif, which is very clear on some examples, suggests strongly that they were made in Syria, where Saint Simeon Stylites and his imitators attracted pilgrims from all parts of Christendom.

Saint Simeon (about 389–459) was expelled from his monastery for excessive austerity and spent the rest of his life perched on a series of pillars (the Greek word for a column is *stylos*; hence stylite, one who stands on a pillar). According to his biographer, Theodoretus, pilgrims visited Simeon from as far afield as Britain and after his death frequented the shrine built around his pillar at Qala'at Sema'an. Pitchers decorated with stylite figures and related vessels, therefore, may have been made as early as the mid-fifth century, when Saint Simeon was already attracting attention; presumably, production ceased with the Arab invasion, if not before it. Thus, they are contemporary with the "Jerusalem" bottles and pitchers, and they probably had a similar function: to serve as pilgrims' souvenirs, perhaps containing oil or water.

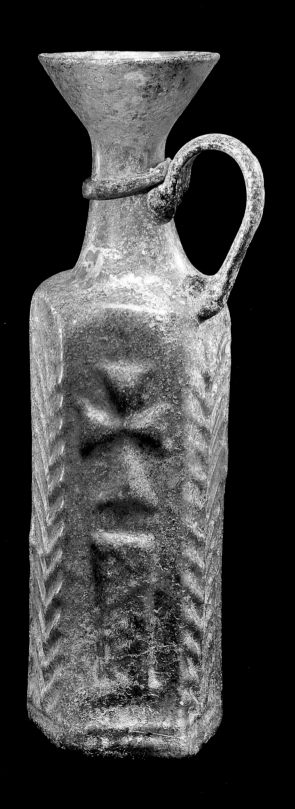

THE COMMONEST METHOD of decorating glass when it was cold consisted of cutting and engraving. We have no direct evidence of the tools used for this purpose by the Romans, although Pliny implies the existence of some kind of rotary instrument. Examination of the glasses themselves shows that the instrument was a lathe. It was employed in two different ways: (1) for mounting and rotating the object while the cutting tool was applied to it (just as a woodworker turns a bowl while applying a chisel), and (2) for mounting and rotating the tool (probably a wheel) while holding the object in the hand. Additional details might have been added by engraving with hand tools tipped with flint and even diamond.

In Roman times, lathes were turned in one of two ways. The more common technique was to use a bow, the string of which was looped around the spindle of the lathe. By moving the bow with a sawing motion, the operator or his assistant rotated the spindle first in one direction and then in the other. An identical reciprocating motion was achieved by using a longer strap or belt, fastened at one end to a weight or supple wooden pole which the operator put under tension by bending. When the weight or the pole was released, the spindle rotated.

Ever since the Renaissance, European engravers have used copper wheels fed with an abrasive paste. In fact, it is the hard grains of the abrasive that cut the glass, not the copper. Roman engravers used the same principle, and Pliny listed some of the abrasives used by craftsmen who worked with semiprecious stones. These included "sand from Naxos" (which is emery), various other sands, and powdered pumice. Emery is an excellent abrasive for cutting glass.

Fig. 19
Bowl, blown and wheel-cut, with the miracle of Christ healing a paralytic. Probably Italy, 4th century A.D. D. 6.3 cm (2½ in). 66.1.38.

All four Gospels describe miracles in which Christ healed persons who were paralyzed. Mark 2:3–12, for example, describes the miracle at Capernaum, where a paralytic lying on a bed was let down from the roof of his house because his friends could not carry him through the crowd around Jesus. Similarly, John 5:3–9 describes a miracle at the pool of Bethesda in Jerusalem. In both cases, the man was healed when Jesus told him to rise and take up his bed. Here, Christ stands on the left. The paralytic walks away, carrying his bed.

THE FRENCH TRAVELER Chardin (1643–1712) wrote a vivid description of the working methods of gem cutters in Iran. He described the use of a lathe and of composite wheels made of emery in a resinous matrix. Although we have no reason to suppose that the Romans made composite wheels, Chardin's description conveys something of the character of gem and glass cutting before the Renaissance: "The Persian lapidaries make their wheels of two parts of emery and one part of lac [a natural resin]. . . . They rotate these wheels hafted on to circular spindles, with a bow which they hold in one hand, while with the other they hold the stone against the wheel. . . . When they want to polish the stone, they put in place of the wheel another made of red willow, on which they throw putty or tripoli [finely powdered silica]. The seal-engravers employ the bow and a very small copper wheel with emery."

More often than not, Roman glassmakers polished the ornament they had made by cutting. Occasionally, however, they left these areas rough to create a contrast between the granular surface of the decoration and the smooth surface of the background. This is known as abrasion. The Populonia Bottle, shown on the opposite page, is an outstanding example of late Roman abraded decoration.

Fig. 20

Bottle, blown and engraved (abraded). Probably Italy, 4th century A.D. H. 18.4 cm (7¼ in). 62.1.31.

The Populonia Bottle is one of a group of nine vessels, all of similar form, decorated with waterfront scenes and inscriptions. The scenes fall into two groups. The first includes a lake, palace, oyster bed, jetty, and columns. The second has an amphitheater, theater, stadium, temple, jetty, and columns. Inscriptions on some examples identify the first group as Baiae, a Roman harbor town and resort on the Bay of Naples, and the second as Puteoli. The Populonia Bottle belongs to the first group and illustrates famous buildings in and around Baiae. Its name records the findspot, Populonia (near modern Piombino) in Tuscany, where it was discovered about 1822.

THE MOST EXCLUSIVE luxury glasses made in the later Roman Empire are known as "cage cups." They were made between about A.D. 250 and the early to mid-fourth century. The earliest datable fragment from a late Roman cage cup was found in Athens, among the debris from a house which is thought to have been destroyed when the Heruli raided the city in 267.

Cage cups were made by the laborious and risky process of cutting and grinding a single thick-walled blank. Breaking just one mesh of the cage meant that the entire vessel had to be written off. We might expect, therefore, that cage cups were special, and at least one had an owner of exceptional importance. This is the cage cup discovered in 1826 at Strasbourg, France, and destroyed in 1870 during the Franco-Prussian War. The Strasbourg beaker had a colorless body, a purple cage, and an emerald-green inscription. The inscription was incomplete, but it may be restored with confidence to read "MAXIMIANE AVGVSTE," a reference to the emperor Maximian, who ruled from 286 to 310. Whether the object was made *for* the emperor, or to be presented as a gift *by* him, we do not know. In either case, however, it shows that cage cups were owned by the most privileged members of Roman society.

Fig. 21
Cage cup, cast or blown, wheel-cut. About A.D. 300. D. 12.1 cm (7¾ in). 87.1.1.

Some cage cups are shaped like beakers and are inscribed with toasts such as "Drink! May you live for many years!" Others, like this example, are shaped like bowls. The metal fittings indicate that, at the time of burial, it was meant to be suspended. This raises the possibility that bowl-shaped cage cups were hanging lamps rather than drinking vessels.

THERE ARE TWO kinds of painted decoration on glass. In the first kind, the surface is covered with watercolor, tempera, or oil paint. This technique is known as cold painting. In the second kind, the "paint" is made from powdered glass and is fused to the surface of the object by means of heating in a furnace. This more permanent technique is known as enameling. The Romans practiced both techniques. The Daphne Ewer, shown on the opposite page, was decorated with cold painting and gilding.

Fig. 22

The Daphne Ewer, blown, with cold-painted and gilded decoration of Apollo, urged on by Desire, pursuing Daphne. Eastern Mediterranean, probably Syria, 3rd century A.D. H. 22.2 cm (8⅜ in). 55.1.86.

In Greek mythology, the nymph Daphne was the daughter of the river god Peneus, or (as in this version) Ladon. She spent her time hunting in the forests, resisting her father's entreaties to take a husband. The god Apollo, wounded by one of the arrows of Pothos (Desire), saw Daphne and fell in love with her. She fled from his attentions and, almost exhausted by the chase, called out to her father to rescue her. The prayer was answered. As Apollo reached out to embrace her, she was transformed into a laurel tree. Here, we see Apollo, urged on by Desire. Daphne is shown on the other side, at the moment of her transformation.

The Daphne Ewer was found at Kerch on the Black Sea coast of the Soviet Union.

PRE-ROMAN GLASSMAKERS had created objects in which gold foil was laminated between two almost identical vessels, one inside the other. A similar effect was achieved in later Roman times, first for medallions bearing portraits and later for roundels at the center of dishes and bowls. The latter, known as "gold glasses," were frequently displayed beside tombs in the catacombs, the underground galleries used by Jews and Christians for burying their dead.

Gold glasses were probably made by applying a sheet of gold foil to a glass disk. The foil was then cut to show the desired subject matter; in a few cases, details were enlivened with paint or enamel. This disk, decorated in gold on the upper surface, formed the base of the vessel. The decoration was protected and the floor and sides of the vessel were formed by fusing a second piece of glass over the first. This was probably done either by heating the two elements in a furnace until they fused (the technique used by pre-Roman glassmakers) or by inflating a bubble of hot glass against the base disk after the latter had been reheated to prevent thermal shock. After inflation, the bubble would have been cut open with shears and removed from the blowpipe. Finally, the wall and rim were shaped by reheating and tooling.

Fig. 23
Gold-glass roundel from the bottom of a vessel. Gold foil sandwiched between two layers of glass. Italy, 4th century A.D. D. 9.7 cm ($3^{13}/_{16}$ in). 66.1.37.

A shepherd tends his flock. The inscriptions surrounding the scene are drinkers' toasts. In translation the inscriptions read, "(Be) the pride of your friends; Drink that you may live; May you live."

THE LAST OBJECT in this book is known as the Disch Kantharos. (A kantharos is a two-handled cup, and Carl Disch was a famous 19th-century collector who once owned the cup shown on the opposite page.) It was made in the third or early fourth century A.D. somewhere in the western provinces of the Roman Empire, possibly at Cologne, and it is of extraordinary interest for several reasons. First, like the gold glasses, it is decorated with gold foil, which was applied to the outside of the cup and then carefully cut away so that only the figures of cupids playing among flowers remained. Unlike the gold glasses, however, the Disch Kantharos has no cover glass to protect the gold. Instead, the maker constructed a "poor man's cage cup" from trails of hot glass.

Fig. 24
Cup with two handles (the Disch Kantharos), blown, with gilded decoration and applied cage and handles. Mediterranean or Germany, 3rd–4th century A.D. H. (surviving) 13.8 cm (5⁷⁄₁₆ in). 66.1.267.

As far as we know, only two objects of this type have come to light: the Disch Kantharos and a "twin" which was last heard of when it was in the collection at Schloss Goluchov in Poland before World War II. In the 19th century, these objects were famous, and a glasshouse at Ehrenfeld, near Cologne, marketed replicas between 1881 and 1886.

The Disch Kantharos is said to have been found in Cologne in 1864.

GLOSSARY

Annealing. The process of gradually cooling an object in an auxiliary part of the glass furnace, or in a separate furnace, so that any strain created in the glass during forming may be eliminated.

Batch. The mixture of raw materials (usually soda, lime, and silica) heated together in a pot or tank to make glass. Minor ingredients, such as colorants, may be added to the batch.

Blank. Any cooled glass object which requires further forming or decorating to be finished.

Blowing. The technique of forming an object by inflating a gob of molten glass gathered on the end of an iron tube, or *blowpipe*. The *gaffer* slightly inflates the gob, manipulates it into the required form by swinging it or rolling it on a *marver* or shaping it with tools or in a mold, and then further inflates it.

Blowpipe. A hollow metal pipe for blowing glass.

Cage cup. A vessel decorated by undercutting so that the surface decoration stands free of the body of the glass, supported by struts. The vessel appears, therefore, to be enclosed in an openwork cage.

Cameo glass. Glass of one color covered, often by *casing*, with one or more layers of contrasting color. The outer layers are carved, cut, or engraved to produce a design which stands out from the background.

Cane. A group of slender rods of glass, groups of which are bundled and fused to form a polychrome design. See also *rod*.

Carving. The removal of glass from the surface of an object by means of hand-held tools such as files, points, gravers, and riffles.

Casing. The application of a layer of glass over a layer of contrasting color. The *gaffer* inflates a *gob* of hot glass inside a pre-cast or blown *blank* of a contrasting color. The two components adhere to each other and are inflated (perhaps with frequent reheating) until they have the requisite form. After *annealing*, the upper layer is carved and cut in relief to produce *cameo* glass.

Core. The form around which molten glass is trailed and wound in order to build a vessel.

Core-forming. The technique of forming a vessel by trailing molten glass around a core supported by a metal rod. After forming, the object was removed from the rod and annealed. After *annealing*, the core was removed by scraping.

Cutting. The decorative technique whereby glass is removed from the surface of an object by grinding with a rotating stone wheel fed with an abrasive suspended in water. See also *carving* and *engraving*.

Diatretum, vas diatretum. (Latin, openwork vessel.) A term frequently used to refer to cage cups.

Engraving. The technique of cutting into the surface of a glass object by holding it against a rotating copper wheel fed with an abrasive. See also *carving* and *cutting*.

Fire-polishing. The reintroduction of a vessel into the furnace to eliminate surface irregularities.

Gaffer. The master glassblower in charge of a workshop.

Gather or gob. A quantity of glass collected on the end of the *blowpipe*.

Glass. A homogeneous material with a random, liquid-like (non-crystalline) molecular structure. The manufacturing process requires that the raw materials be heated to a temperature sufficient to cause a completely fused melt which, when cooled rapidly, becomes rigid without crystallizing.

Lathe-cutting. The technique whereby a *blank* in the general shape of the finished object is mounted and (in antiquity) turned with the aid of a bow or handled wheel, while a tool fed with abrasive is held against the surface in order to polish it or to modify the profile.

Marver. A smooth, flat surface, over which softened glass is rolled in order to smooth the vessel wall or consolidate trailed decoration.

Millefiori. (Italian, a thousand flowers.) *Mosaic glass.*

Mold blowing. Inflating a *parison* of hot glass in a reusable mold. The glass is forced against the inner surfaces of the mold and assumes its shape, together with any decoration that it bears.

Mosaic glass. Objects made from preformed elements placed in a mold and heated until they fuse.

Overlay. A layer of glass which covers a layer of a different color, often as the result of *casing*.

Parison, paraison. A gather, on the end of a *blowpipe*, which is already slightly inflated.

Polishing. Smoothing the surface of an object when it is cold by holding it against a rotating wheel fed with an abrasive, such as emery.

Pontil. A solid metal rod, usually tipped with a wad of hot glass, which is applied to the base to hold the vessel during manufacture. It usually leaves a scar—a pontil mark—on the base when it is removed.

Reheating. The act of softening a partly formed vessel by reintroducing it into the furnace, while it is attached to the *blowpipe* or *pontil*.

Rod. A monochrome segment of glass cut from a trail.

Tooling. Shaping hot glass with tools such as tongs and pincers.

Trail. A strand of glass, roughly circular in section, drawn out from a *gather*.

Weathering. Changes on the surface of glass caused by chemical reaction with the environment.

FURTHER READING

The Roman Empire

Cornell, Tim, and Matthews, John. *Atlas of the Roman World*. New York: Facts on File, Inc., [about 1983].

Cunliffe, Barry. *Rome and Her Empire*. Maidenhead, England: McGraw-Hill Book Company, 1978.

Studies on Roman Glass

Grose, David. "The Formation of the Roman Glass Industry." *Archaeology*, v. 36, no. 4, July/August 1983, pp. 38–45.

"The Origins and Early History of Glass." In *The History of Glass*, edited by Dan Klein and Ward Lloyd. London: Orbis, 1984, pp. 9–37.

Harden, D. B. "Ancient Glass, II: Roman." *Archaeological Journal*, v. 126, 1970, pp. 44–66.

Price, Jennifer. "Glass." In *Roman Crafts*, edited by Donald Strong and David Brown. London: Duckworth, 1976, pp. 111–125.

"Glass." In *A Handbook of Roman Art*, edited by Martin Henig. London: Phaidon, 1983, pp. 205–219.

Catalogs of Collections and Exhibitions

Auth, Susan H. *Ancient Glass at the Newark Museum*. Newark, N.J.: Newark Museum, 1976.

Goldstein, Sidney M. *Pre-Roman and Early Roman Glass in The Corning Museum of Glass*. Corning, N.Y.: The Corning Museum of Glass, 1979.

Harden, D. B.; Hellenkemper, H.; Painter, K.; and Whitehouse, D. *Glass of the Caesars*. Milan: Olivetti, 1987.

Harden, D. B.; Painter, K. S.; Pinder-Wilson, R. H.; and Tait, H. *Masterpieces of Glass*. London: The Trustees of The British Museum, 1968.

Hayes, John W. *Roman and Pre-Roman Glass in the Royal Ontario Museum*. Toronto: Royal Ontario Museum, 1975.

Matheson, Susan B. *Ancient Glass in the Yale University Art Gallery*. New Haven, Conn.: Yale University Art Gallery, 1980.